$/00

HUMANOID REX *by Jim Harter. A collage made from illustrations in this book.*

PICTURE SOURCEBOOK
FOR
COLLAGE AND DECOUPAGE

EDITED BY

Edmund V. Gillon, Jr.

WITH INTRODUCTIONS BY
Jean-Claude Suarès
AND Eleanor Hasbrouck Rawlings

DOVER PUBLICATIONS, INC., NEW YORK

Published in Canada by General Publishing Company, Ltd., 30 Lesmill Road, Don Mills, Toronto,
Ontario.
Published in the United Kingdom by Constable
and Company, Ltd.

Picture Sourcebook for Collage and Decoupage
is a new work, first published by Dover Publications, Inc., in 1974.

DOVER *Pictorial Archive* SERIES

International Standard Book Number: 0-486-23095-3
Library of Congress Catalog Card Number: 74-82206

Manufactured in the United States of America
Dover Publications, Inc.
31 East 2nd Street
Mineola, N.Y. 11501

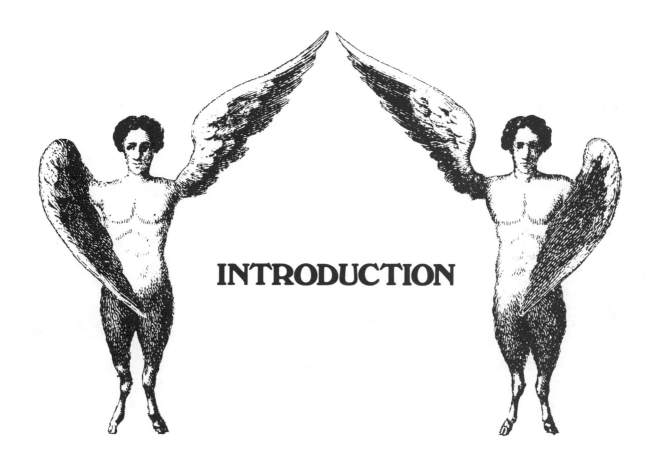

INTRODUCTION

The primary task of the worker in collage and decoupage, the two arts described below by experts in the respective fields, is to find suitable artwork. This book is an attempt to fill that need. It is not a manual, but a sourcebook with essential information. Over 300 sharply defined line cuts, printed clearly, one side only, on paper of suitable weight, comprise a universe of fanciful and provocative notions. Eight pages of these items are in color. Also included are 25 full-page scenes—landscapes, cityscapes, interiors —that can be used as backgrounds for your collages.

What we have provided here is more unusual types of material, which you might have difficulty finding elsewhere and which might prove to be expensive. Naturally, you should also include in your collages such readily available material as snapshots and items from newspapers and magazines. Try antique shops and secondhand bookstores for inexpensive old publications that you can cut up. You will also find a vast amount of suitable material in books belonging to the Dover Pictorial Archive Series.

As an additional aid and stimulus to the beginner, this volume also contains a selection of completed collages, many created chiefly with elements to be found in this book.

Collage

by *Jean-Claude Suarès*

WHAT IS IT?

Collage is the art that consists of cutting out and pasting down. The word is derived from the French verb *coller,* "to glue." Since the images used in collages already exist, the function of the artist is to select and rearrange them to fit his own vision.

The world of collage is infinite. In what other art form can you look for a specific image, for example, combine it with one you have found by accident, and paste them on the front page of your morning newspaper, and watch them all become a whole new concept?

The birth of collage can be traced back to the

Collage by Max Ernst from UNE SEMAINE DE BONTÉ OU LES SEPT ÉLÉMENTS CAPITAUX, *1934.*

fall of 1912, when Picasso and Braque began to incorporate bits of newsprint, wrapping paper, wallpaper, playing cards and cigarette wrappers into their paintings. Later on, toward the end of the period of Synthetic Cubism, Picasso, Braque and Juan Gris began cutting out elements with scissors and creating their works entirely with these bits of paper instead of paint. Collage (*papiers collés*) was invented by the Cubists as a shortcut in achieving textural effects. For example, instead of drawing a comb across wet oil paint to define a certain area of a violin, Braque used a piece of corrugated paper in order to create the same effect in an area of a banjo.

It must be understood that these first collages were really paintings in which bits of paper or cloth simply replaced areas of oil paint. This is why the Cubists lost interest in collage in less than two years. But in the process they had opened our eyes to textures and colors that were formerly considered commonplace.

It was not until the advent of Dadaism and Futurism that collage was rediscovered, but this time to serve an entirely different purpose: the creation of fantastic and absurd images. Dada itself was divided into two movements, one stressing form (Hans Arp and Kurt Schwitters) and the other stressing subject matter (Marcel Duchamp and Max Ernst) —the latter leading into Surrealism.

By gluing, nailing and screwing in his "inartistic" materials, Schwitters created a form of collage unparalleled before in its beauty and uniqueness. He used nothing but worthless objects, mostly collected out of trash cans: pieces of wood, scraps of metal, bits of paper, theater tickets, nails, buttons and pieces of cloth. Things we see every day but never look at became part of the most harmonious compositions of the twentieth century. And all this by someone who had never proven himself much of a conventional painter!

Max Ernst created the link between collage and Surrealism merely by his choice of elements. When old steel engravings, charts and symbols were cut out and then glued or superimposed and given titles like "The gramineous bicycle garnished with bells the pilfered greybeards and the echinoderms bending the spine to look for caresses," the result was "shock through paradox," as John Canaday describes Surrealism. Kurt Schwitters was attacked by this school of Dadaists for the purity and clarity of his collages—one of the features of his work that has made it survive as great art.

From collage emerged the photomontage, which consists mostly of juxtaposing photographs and other reproductions into compositions. There is a great deal of montage in advertisements and in film and television.

HOW IS IT DONE?

MATERIALS. The basic materials of collage are glue and scissors. It is imperative to cut out the elements of a collage with great care. Some artists find it more effective to use razor blades instead of scissors. The best scissors for the purpose are small steel ones, like those found in manicure sets. The best razor blades are the single-edge variety, which can usually be obtained in boxes of 100 at art-supply stores, and cost in the neighborhood of two for a penny.

There are dozens of glues on the market but you must look for one that is transparent and nonstaining. If you are doing your collage on paper or cardboard, you may find it best to use rubber cement. For other surfaces you must use a stronger glue, which may eventually eat through the paper and form stains.

The longest-lasting kind of rubber cement is the "one-coat" formula, a strong adhesive that has to dry first on the bit of paper before you apply it to the collage surface. When working with rubber cement, you should also have at your disposal rubber cement thinner, which dissolves the cement without dissolving the ink, and which evaporates very quickly. You will also need a rubber cement remover or "pick-up," to clean off cement that gets onto the picture surface.

Rubber cement eventually loses its flexibility and crumbles (in about five years). Casein glue (like "Elmer's"), made from milk, reacts chemically with inks and discolors them. Synthetic adhesives are generally too strong and shrink the paper. Vegetable glues made from starches or dextrins seem like the best bet for longevity. It is a vegetable glue, gum arabic, that is used on stamps—which never fall off their envelopes.

More important than your choice of glue is proper gluing. The surfaces, which must be clean, should be covered thoroughly with as thin a layer of glue as possible: the strength of a properly bonded joint is much greater than that of a larger amount of glue. After the collage is done, it should be protected from moisture and high temperatures.

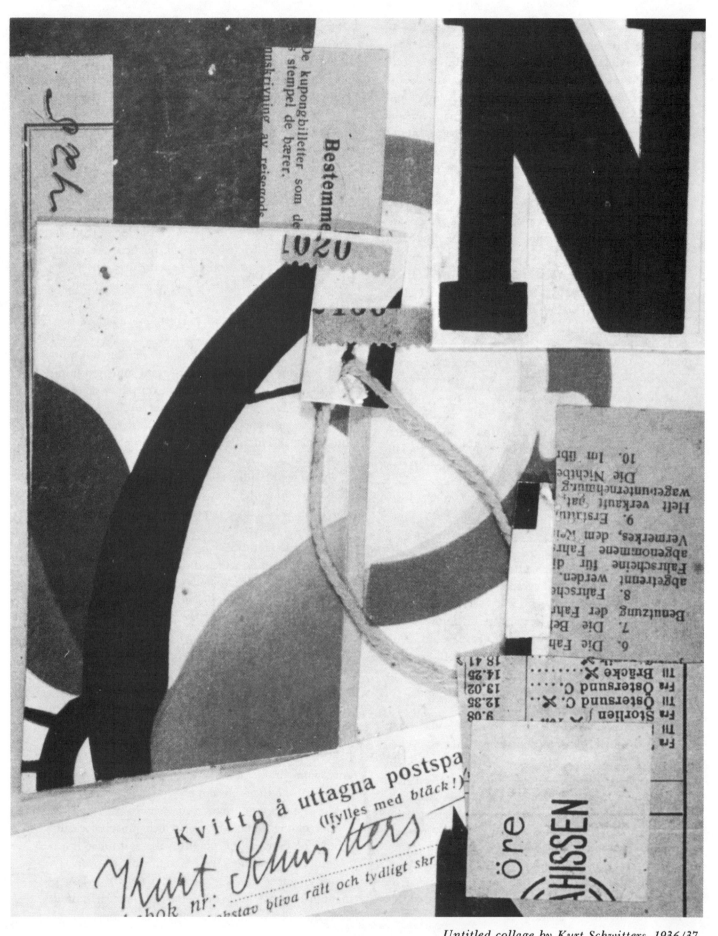

Untitled collage by Kurt Schwitters, 1936/37.

COMPOSITION.   The composition of a collage, in principle, is no different from that of any other work of art. You need a general point of view or theme. You need a dominant element, a dominant direction, a dominant color, and all these need subdominants. In other words, even if you choose nothing but two pieces of corrugated cardboard to design your collage, they should vary in size or they will fight for attention and eventually cancel each other out. This principle of dominance also holds true for the movement of the elements and for the color combinations.

Unity can be achieved by pairing materials that are similar in manufacture as opposed to subject. Two rabbits, one steel-engraved on paper and the other cut out of metal, are not likely to combine well. But two steel engravings, one of a rabbit and the other of a hunter, are almost sure to harmonize.

The images in this book can be used in abstract compositions, in surrealistic visions or in purely decorative designs. If you place an object in a bare landscape and draw a horizon line in the distance, you have basic Surrealism. When the same object is placed on a table in a room, it takes on a whole new meaning. Place it in the sky and it has changed the whole atmosphere of that picture. That same object, repeated in a grid pattern, may become more and more interesting by mere repetition. Sometimes the simplest collages can have an incredible impact (a moustache on the *Mona Lisa*). Sometimes the mere crowding of elements in a given area can cause a holocaust. By simply placing an object where it does not "belong" (a rock in the sky) you can create a mind-boggling image.

Untitled collage by Anita Siegel. Reproduced courtesy of the artist.

WHEN JOHNNY COMES MARCHING HOME *by Anita Siegel. Reproduced courtesy of the artist.*

SATURDAY'S MOTHER *by Anita Siegel. Reproduced courtesy of the artist.*

PIECE OF MIND *by Shaun Johnston.*

A POLITICAL STATEMENT 1973 *by Diana Oliver Turner.*

THE UNEXPECTED VISIT by Diana Oliver Turner.

PLANET LAUGHTER by Jim Harter. A collage made from illustrations in this book.

Decoupage

by *Eleanor Hasbrouck Rawlings*

WHAT IS IT?

Decoupage is the art of decorating objects permanently with paper cutouts that have been chosen to satisfy artistic and symbolic purposes. The word is derived from the French verb *decouper,* "to cut out." A decoupage can be *on* wood, metal, glass or ceramic, submerged under many coats of varnish, or *under* glass, where no varnish is required. Even some plastics can be embellished by decoupage, if compatible materials are used.

The art of decoupage as we know it was the invention of Venetian cabinetmakers in the seventeenth century, when there was a great vogue for lacquered furniture from the Orient as well as for pieces painted and gilded by Italian artists. Unable to meet all the demands, cabinetmakers had the wanted designs copied by the fine engravers of their city. These paper prints were hand-colored by apprentices, then applied in gay profusion to cabinets, secretaries, commodes and chairs. Twenty or more coats of lacquer, followed by periodic sanding and polishing, produced an incomparable finish.

Decoupage eventually spread to France, England and Germany, and stimulated a thriving business for cabinetmakers, artists and printers. It became a favorite pastime for royalty and nobility at the court of Louis XVI. In each succeeding century it has seen a renewal. With the wealth of prints and improved finishes available today, it continues to have appeal as a hobby or an art.

Those who desire to create a decoupage must have, or develop, the patience to give meticulous attention to its craftsmanship. Anyone who knows how to cut skillfully with scissors, to glue, to varnish and to sand, can decoupage an object satisfactorily. There are some who will go further; with imagination, taste and a passion for perfection, they will produce pieces of heirloom quality. A very few, who possess all of these assets, and that elusive something more, will create works of art.

HOW IS IT DONE?

The traditional method requires 24 hours after each coat of varnish, but there are also new methods using quick-drying lacquers and plastic finishes. Handicraft shops sell booklets describing these shorter methods, which are excellent for some projects. It would be impossible to describe each of these techniques and their media here. The lasting beauty of the traditional method is a better-known quantity, tested by time, so a summary follows.

It is wise for a beginner to choose a simple object. An unfinished wooden plaque with a molding around the edge fills this requirement. Fill holes or scratches with wood filler; let dry; sand smooth. Seal with sealer solution; let dry about 30 minutes. Rub smooth with #000 steel wool; wipe off all residue with tack cloth. Paint with 3 coats of background color, allowing 24 hours after each coat; sand lightly. The molding can be painted a darker shade for accent. Apply a coat of sealer; let dry about 30 minutes.

Plan your composition around a central theme with a focal point. Proportion, line, balance and color harmony must all be considered for a pleasing result. Experiment with your design until it satisfies you, using Plasti-Tak, a temporary adhesive plastic, to make it stay in place.

PRINTS AND COLORING. Prints from many sources can be combined, but they should be artistically compatible and of a similar technique. Many of the pictures in this book are suitable; the paper on which it is printed takes oil pencil coloring well and, being thin, requires fewer coats of varnish. Greeting cards, wrapping papers, old children's books, programs, nature books—all are rich in material, and are often precolored. Avoid photographs, newspaper, and magazine prints with shiny surfaces or printing on the reverse side. If your print is black and white, like most of those in this book, you may wish to color it. Good-quality colored pencils with an oil base are the best coloring media for decoupage. They are easy to handle, blend well and can be erased if necessary.

SEALING. Seal the print with a solution of ½ alcohol and ½ white shellac, on the face of the print. This keeps the colors from running and reinforces the paper. Dab the solution on quickly in sections and blot it off. Let it dry 30 minutes. To peel a print that is too thick, dampen the back with a sponge. A print on thick paper requires too many coats of varnish to submerge it.

CUTTING. Cutting techniques are important. Use fine, sharp cuticle scissors. Cut away excess paper for better maneuvering. Cut inside areas first so there is more to hold on to. Cut the figures of the design in silhouette; eliminate backgrounds or unwanted details. Do not leave white edges.

GLUING. Lay print on wax paper face down. Apply slow-drying decoupage mucilage sparingly, but thoroughly. Some prefer to spread the glue on the plaque, and then to place the print. After placing the print, press down on it with a slightly damp sponge from the center out to remove excess glue. Do not rub. It also helps if you place wax paper over the glued-down print and roll it with a brayer or wallpaper roller. Spots of glue turn brown under varnish, so clean off every speck with a damp sponge, rinsing the sponge often. Press out any air. Let dry 24 hours. Press all edges of the print firmly with a burnishing tool or your fiingernail to flatten them into the background paint before varnishing.

VARNISHING. Varnish in a dust-free room, never on a damp or rainy day. Wait 24 hours after each coat. One coat can be applied to the face of the plaque in the morning, one to the back at night. The back need not have more than 5 coats. Before applying each coat, stir the varnish thoroughly, but gently. Flow it on generously, but smoothly, with a 1″ sable brush. Remove drips with sandpaper, hairs with a pin. Wrap your brush in aluminum foil and keep it in the freezer between coats. Clean it in a brush cleaner, such as Cabot's, and wash it with soap and water after you are all finished with the varnishing.

SANDING. Some découpeurs start to sand after 10 coats of varnish. You will be less likely to sand through to your print if you apply 20. Dip a 3″ by 2″ piece of #320 Trimite wet/dry sandpaper into a small bowl of detergent suds, fold it over the sanding block, and sand the area over the print to reduce the coats of varnish over it down to the level of the background somewhat. Wipe off the milky residue with a damp towel as needed. Be very careful not to sand all the way through to the print, but if you do, a touch-up can be made with colored pencils. Repeat the process over the whole face of the plaque with #400 Trimite, taking down the varnish over the print still more. Continue until the finish is uniformly smooth, and no edges of the print can be felt or seen. Repeat the process with #600 Trimite and suds. You may need to add as many as ten more coats of varnish if the print has not been submerged. Repeat sanding.

For a final finish the plaque can be rubbed down with a mixture of 2 tablespoons each of raw linseed oil and pumice, then raw linseed oil and rottenstone. A piece of chamois is used for this. Polish with Goddard's Wax, attach a hook, and voilà!

Other suggested projects are: boxes of all shapes and sizes, trays, mirrors, waste bakets, napkin rings, furniture of all sizes, door frames, wall panels, screens, mantelpieces, lamps, shades, vases, ashtrays, purses, picnic baskets, mailboxes, desk accessories, rocks, jewelry, wig stands, picture frames, etc. etc.

After you have completed a few projects and become a lifelong decoupage fan, you will want to obtain one or more of the following books which discuss basic and advanced techniques in detail and provide unlimited inspiration.

Harrower, Dorothy. *Decoupage.* Barrows and Co., 1958.

Linsley, Leslie. *Decoupage, a New Look at an Old Craft.* Doubleday, 1972.

Manning, Hiram. *Manning on Decoupage.* Hearthside Press, 1969.

Newman, Thelma R. *Contemporary Decoupage.* Crown, 1972.

Nimocks, Patricia E. *Decoupage.* Scribner's, 1968.

Sommer, Elyse. *Decoupage Old and New.* Watson-Guptill, 1971.

Wing, Frances S. *Complete Book of Decoupage.* Coward-McCann, 1965.

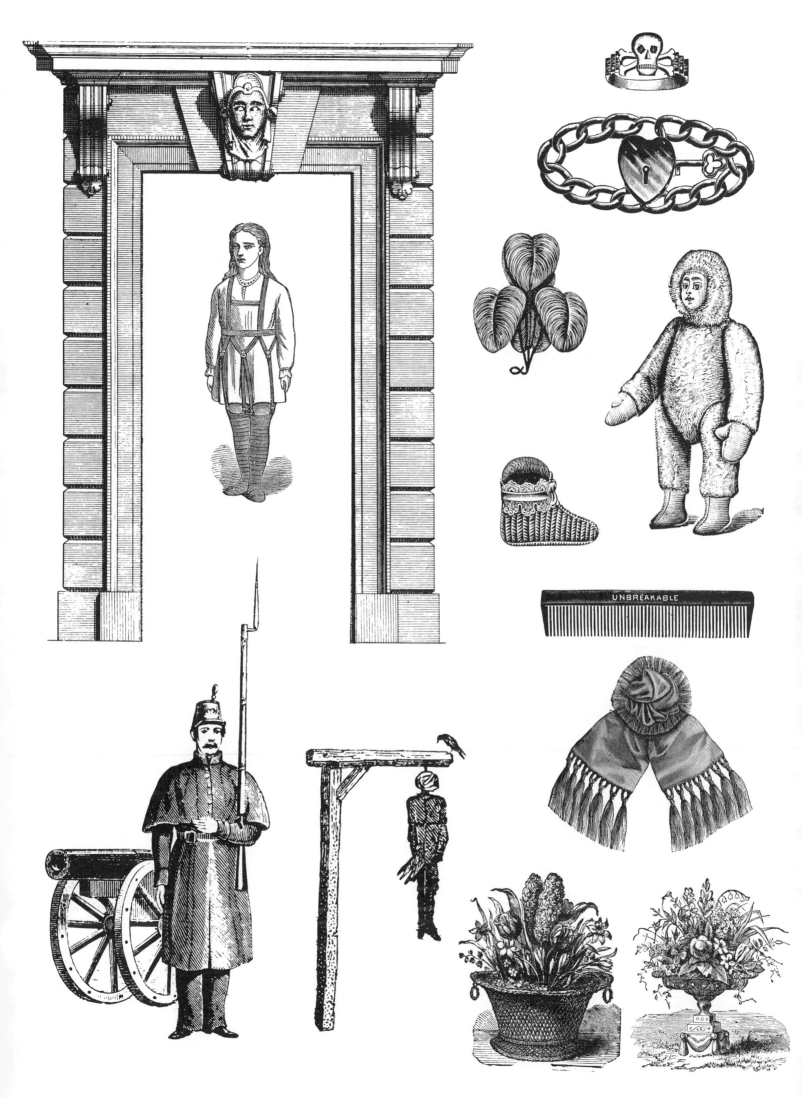

11

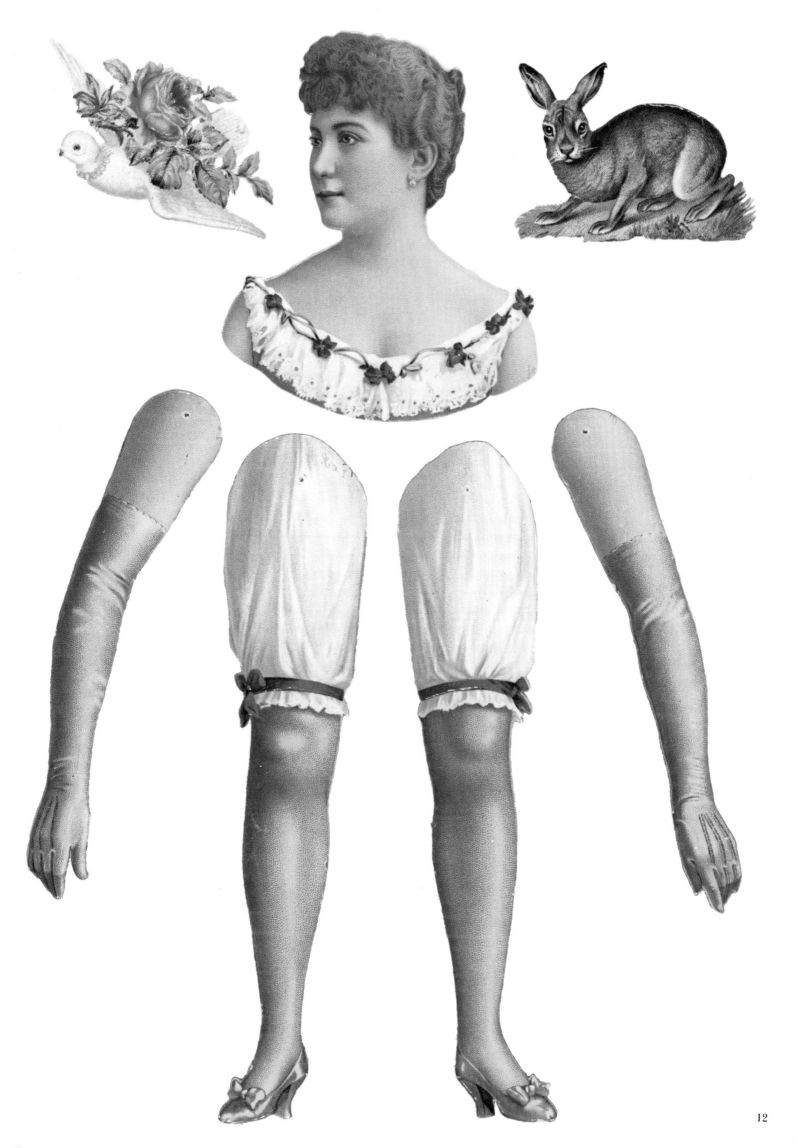

FOR HUMANITY
AND CIVILIZATION

DER CAPTAIN
RED NOSE ~ BLACK MUSTACHE
BLACK CAP ~ BRASS BUTTONS
GREEN CAP ~ BRASS BUTTONS
RED TROUSERS ~ SHOES ~

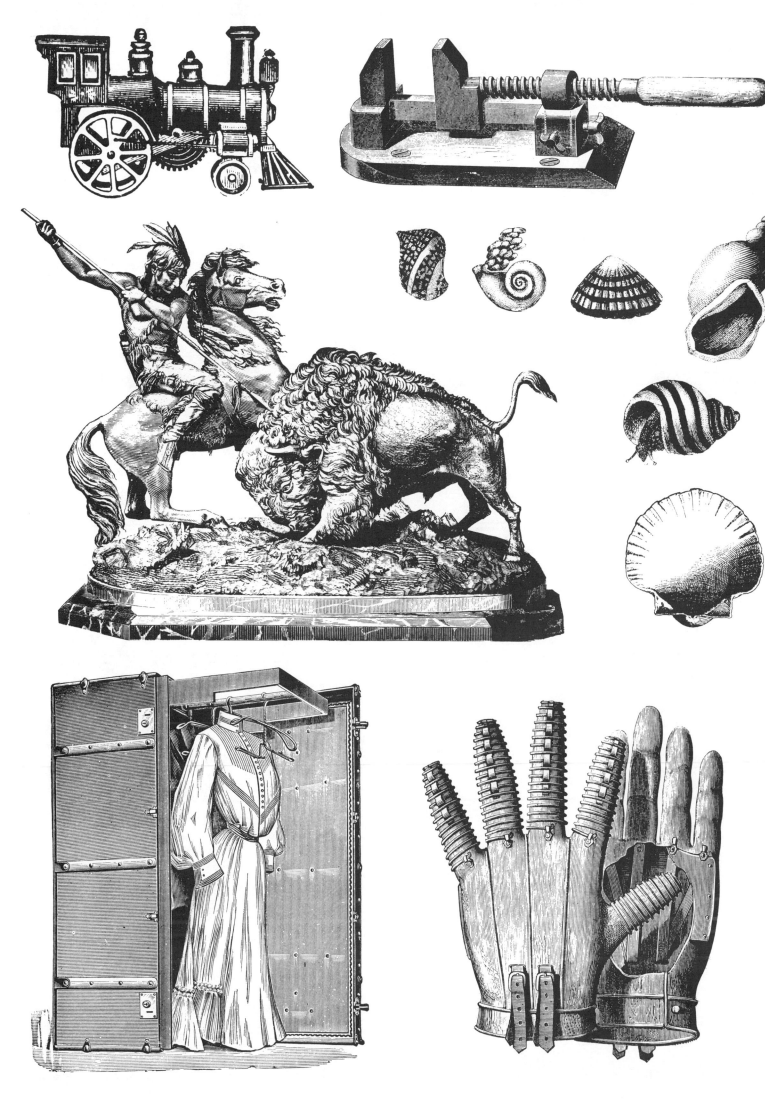

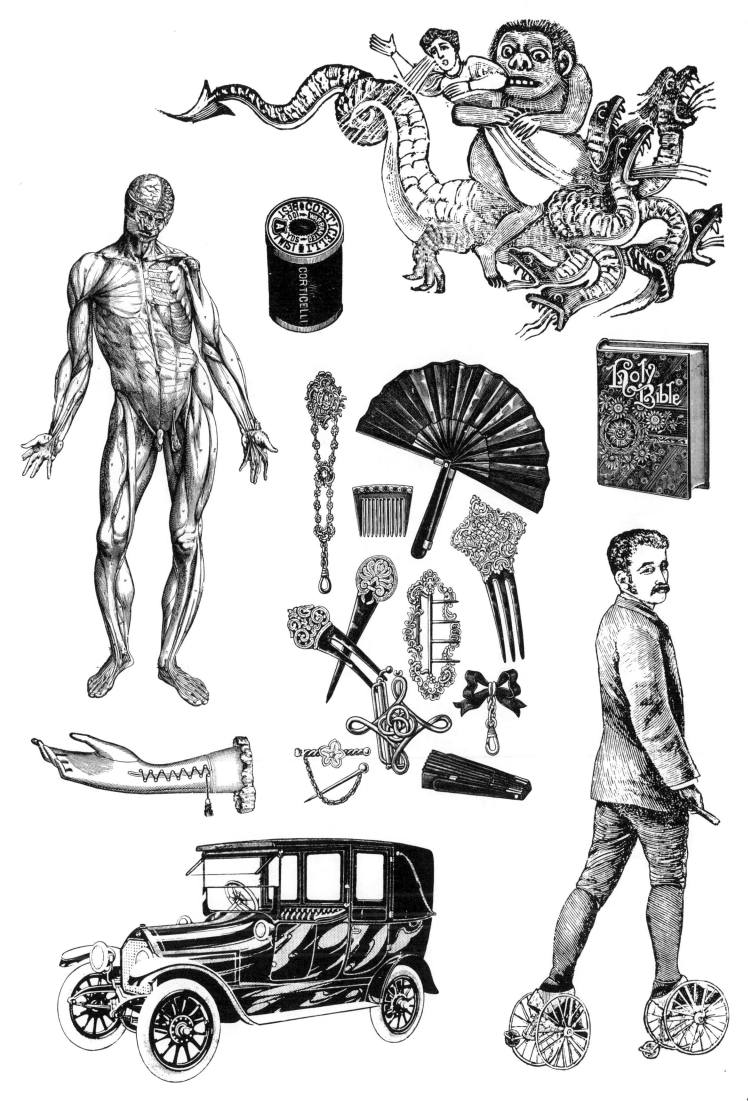

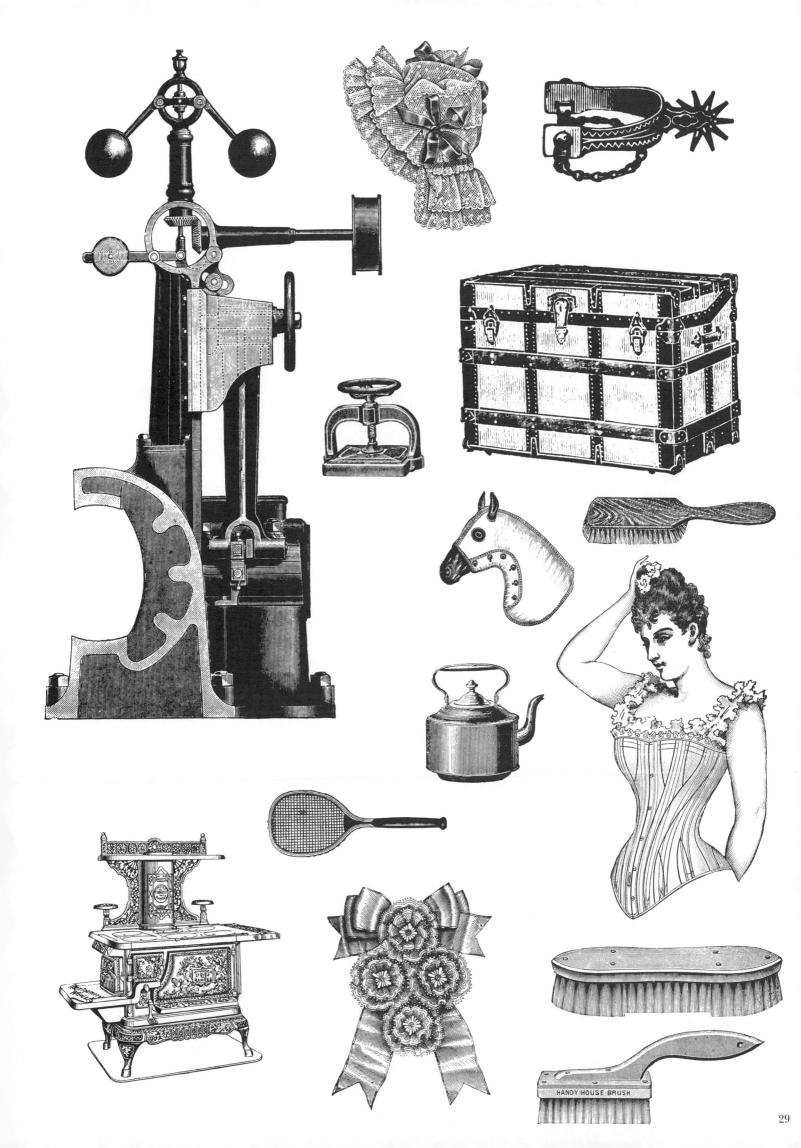

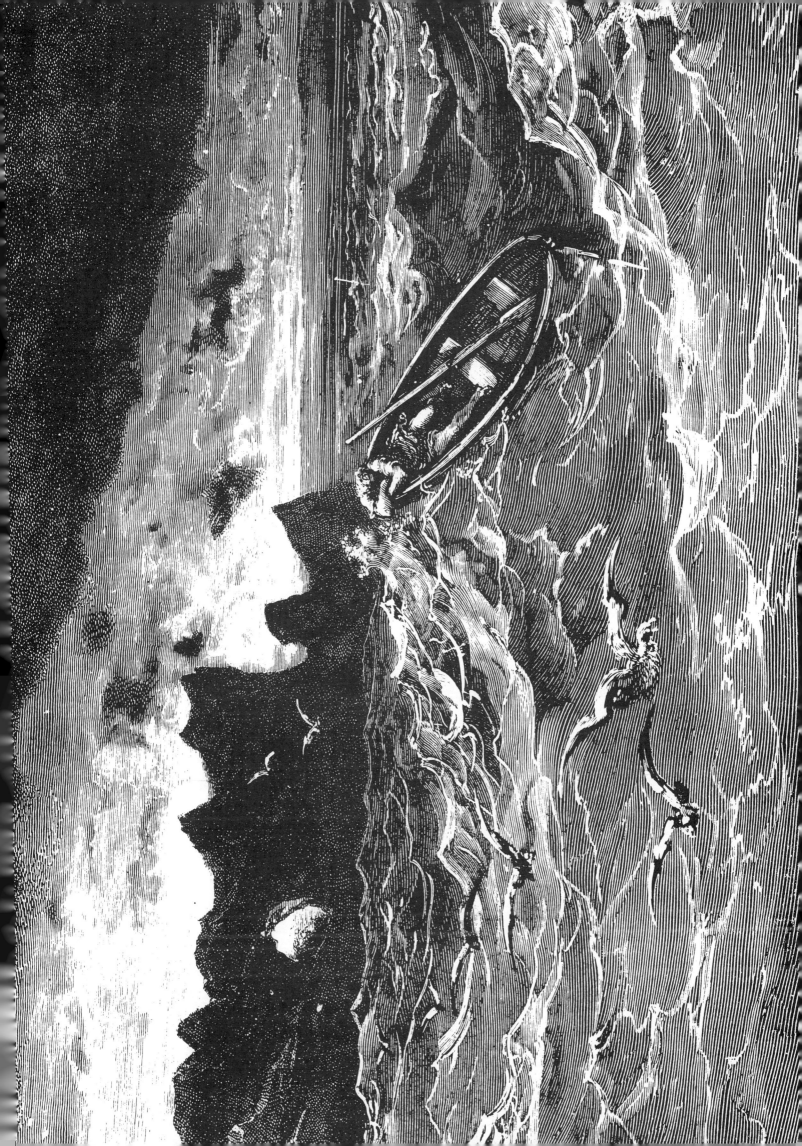

31

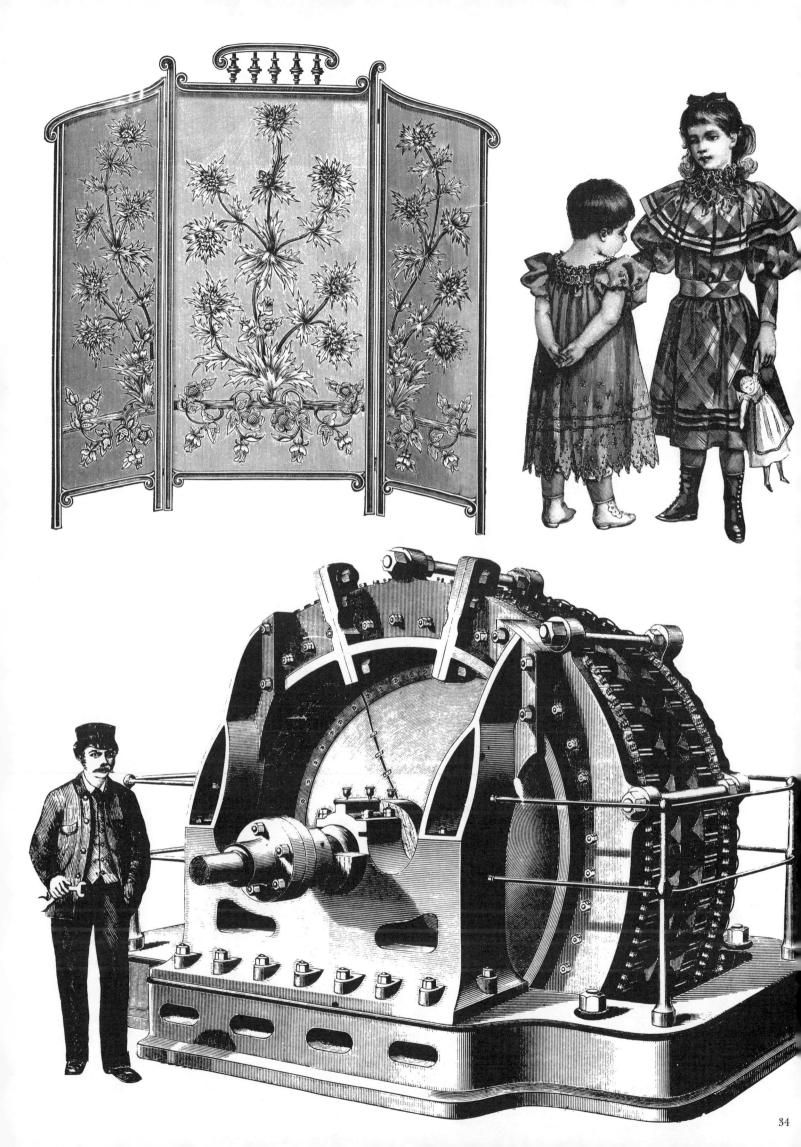

35

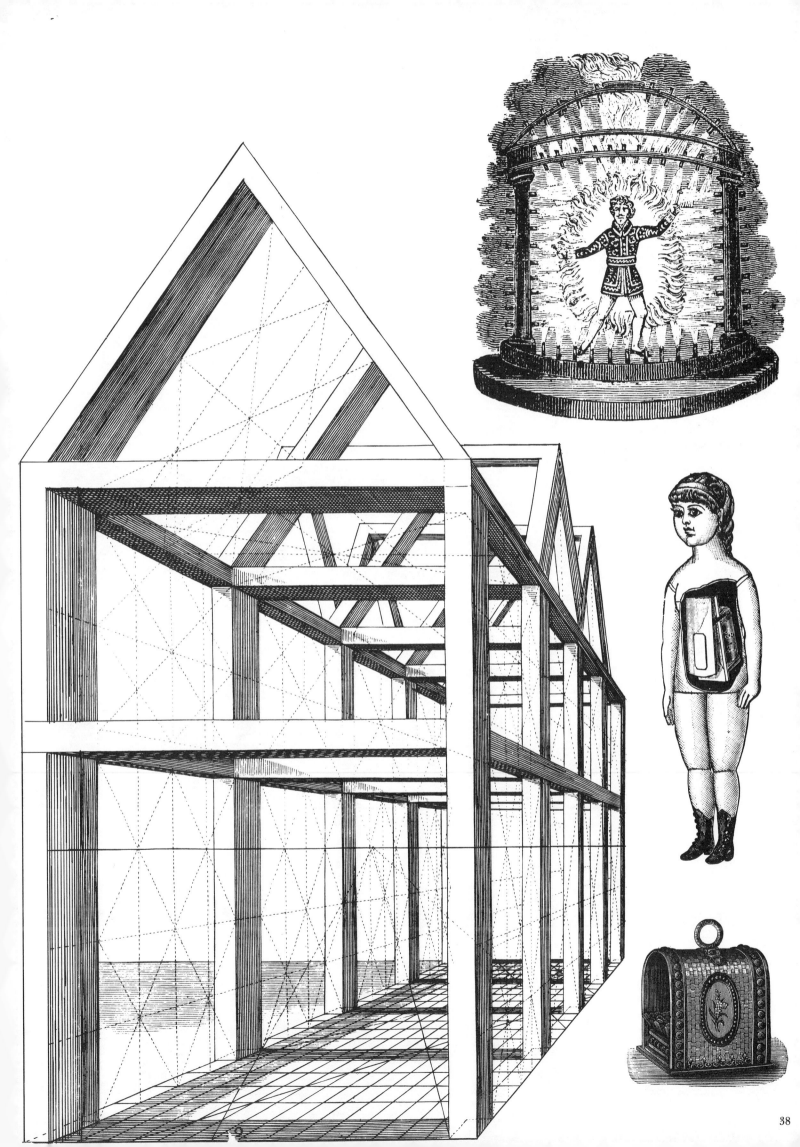

38

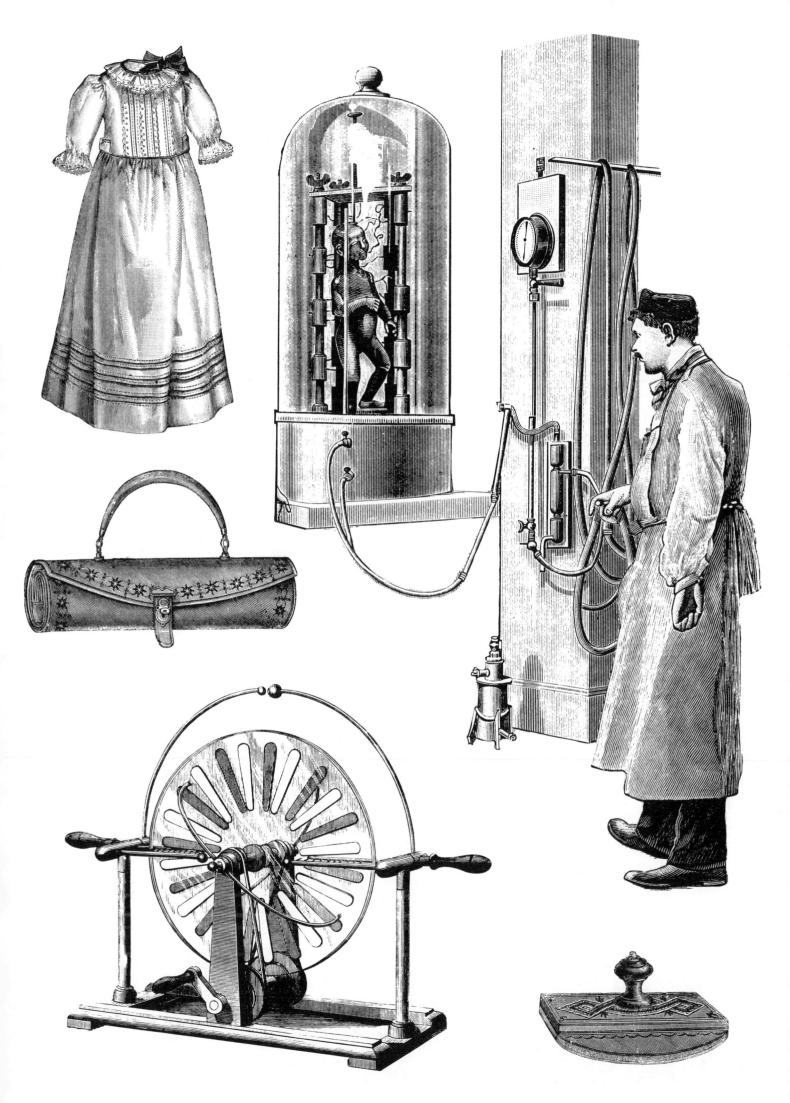

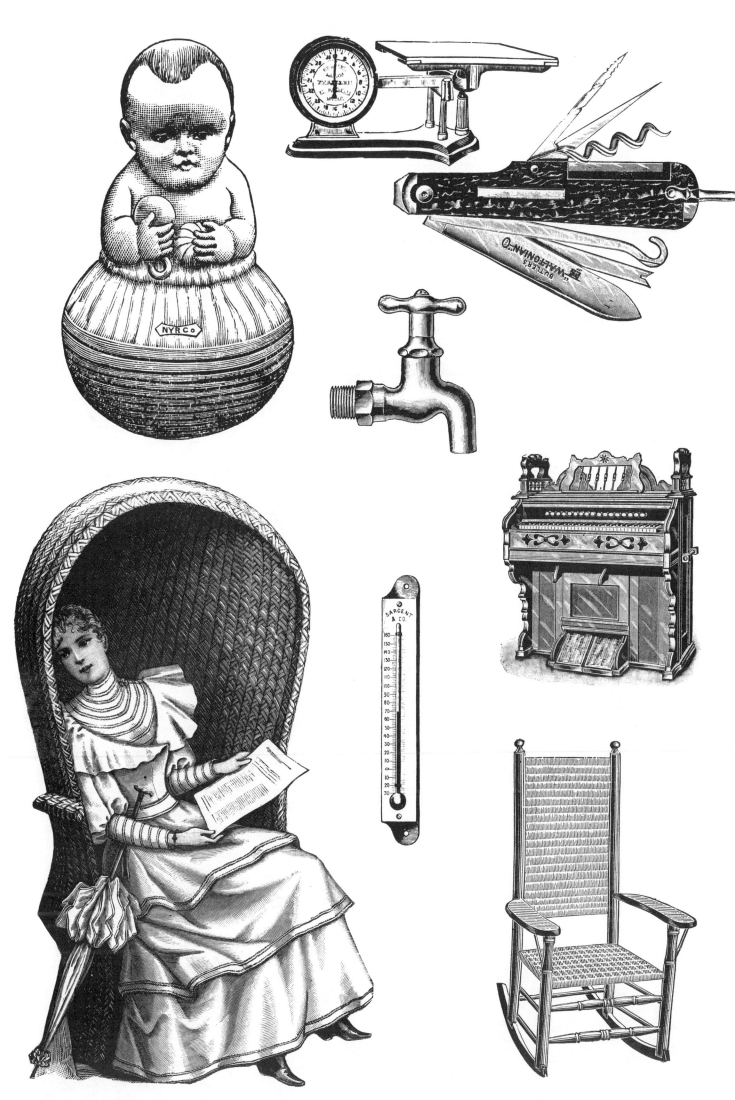

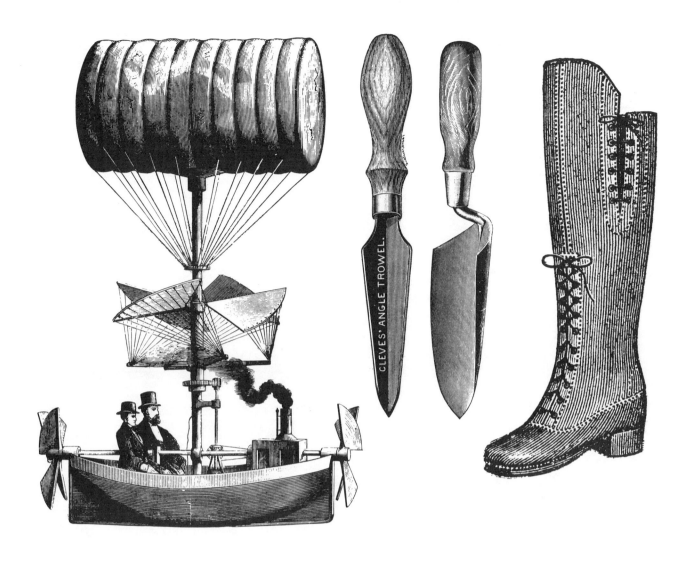

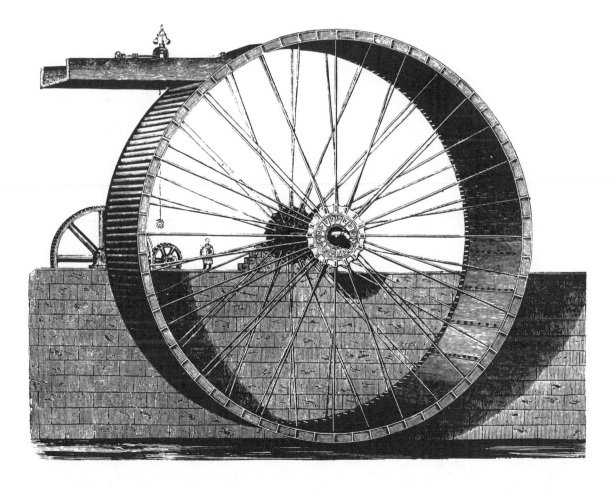

Picture Sourcebook For Collage & Decoupage

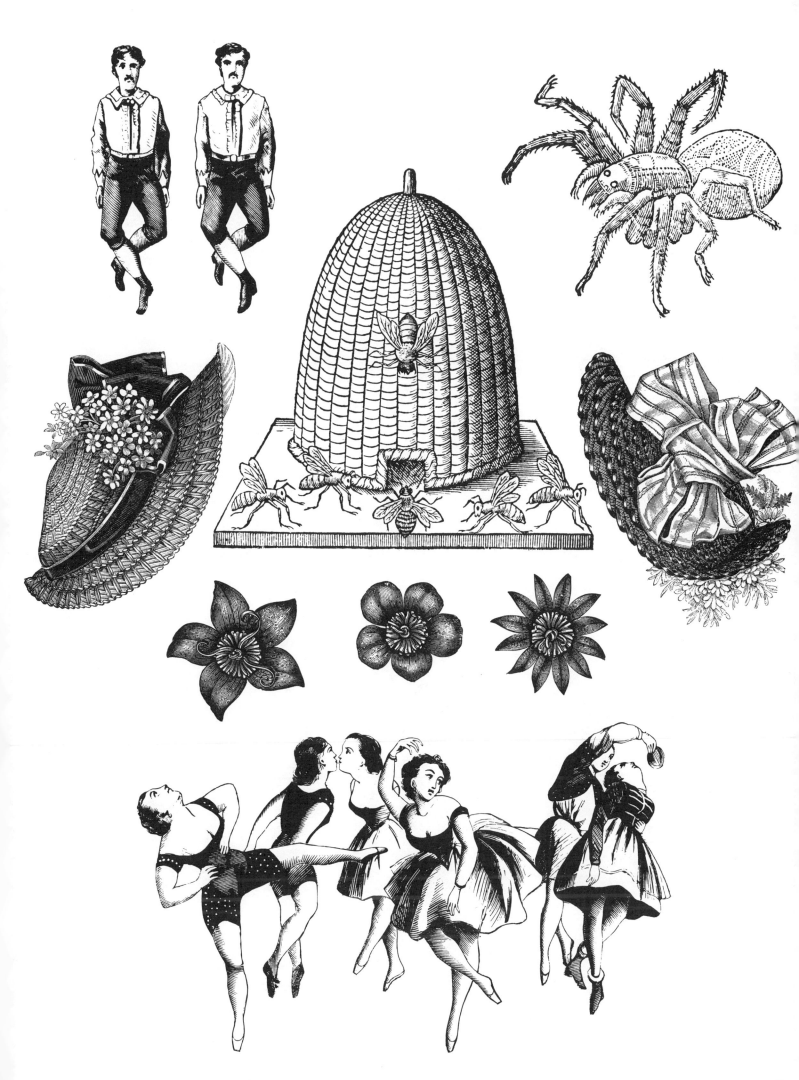

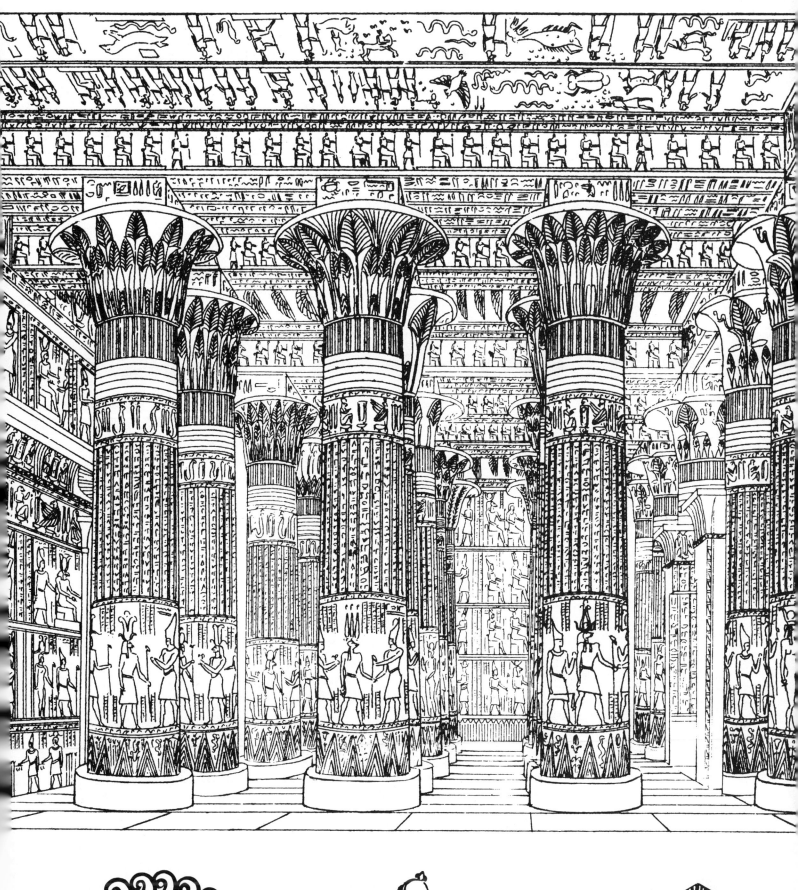

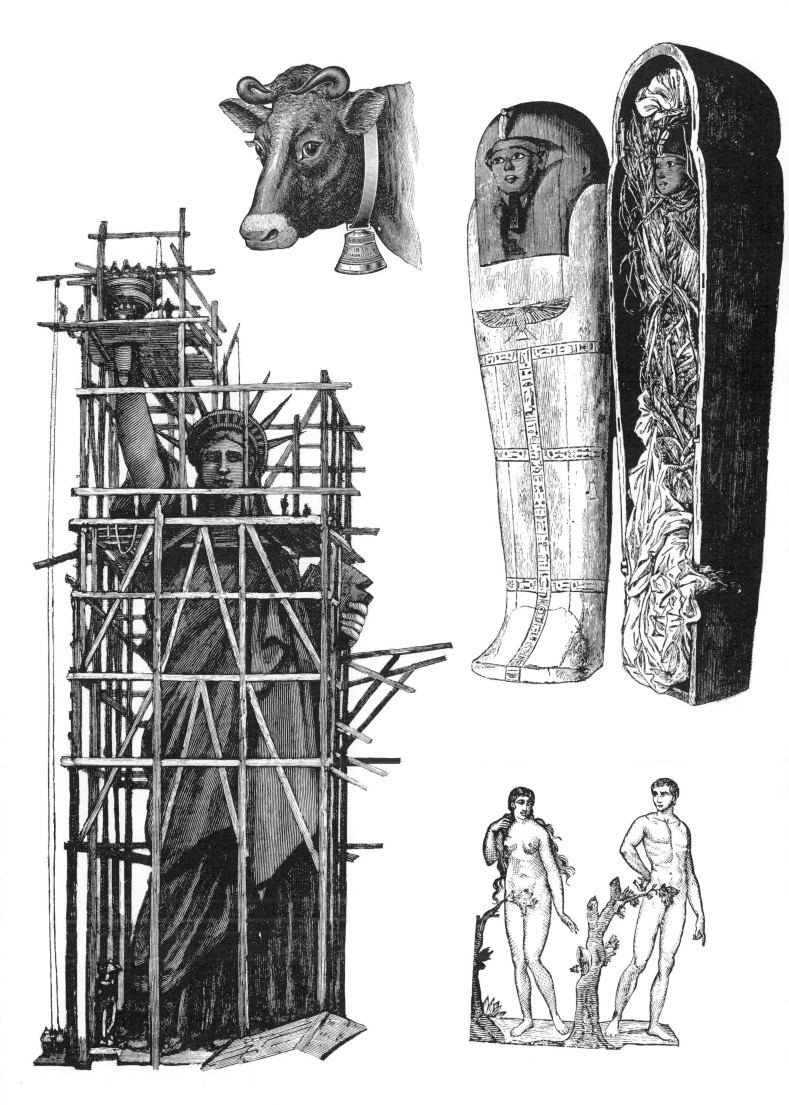

5

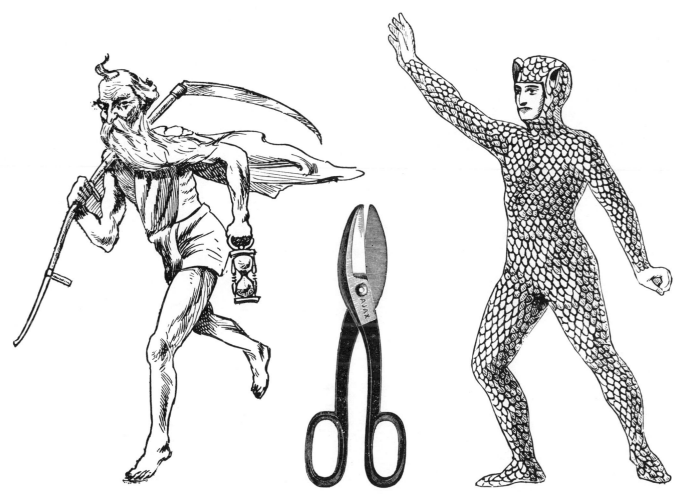

COFFEE ROASTED DAILY.

SPRECKLEY

100, STOKES CROFT

THE STORES.

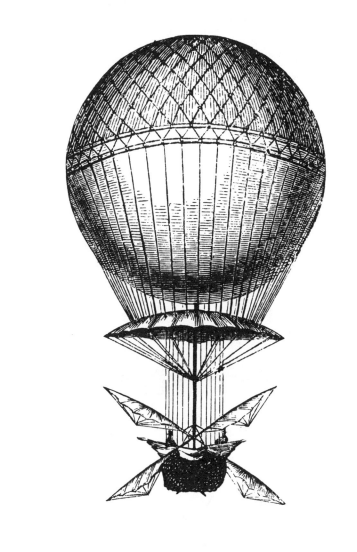

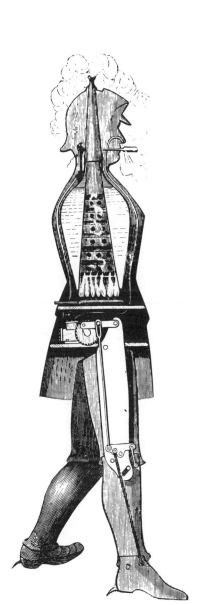

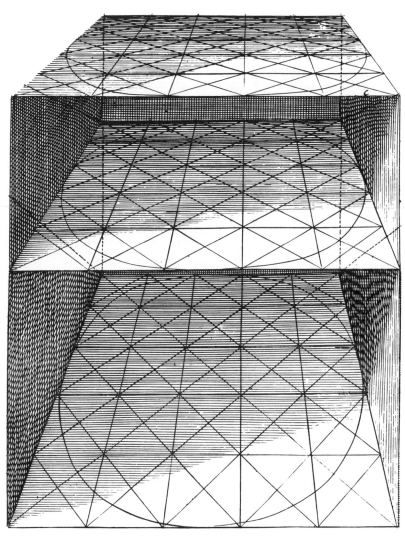

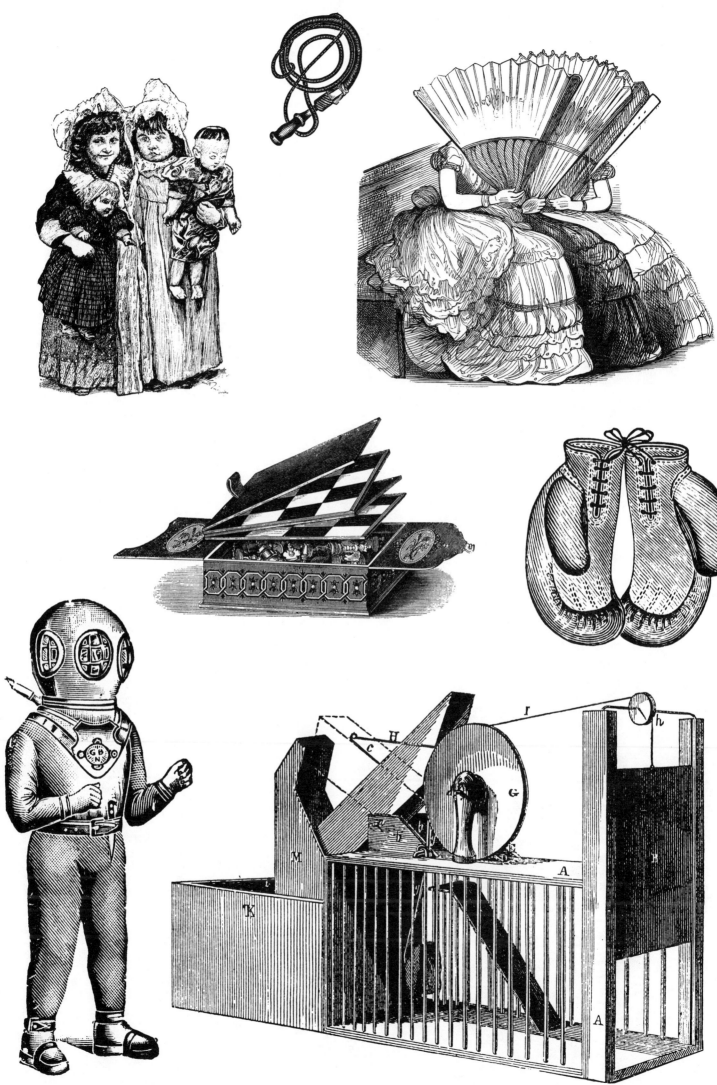

KORRECT SHAPE.

Burt&Packard

Orizon

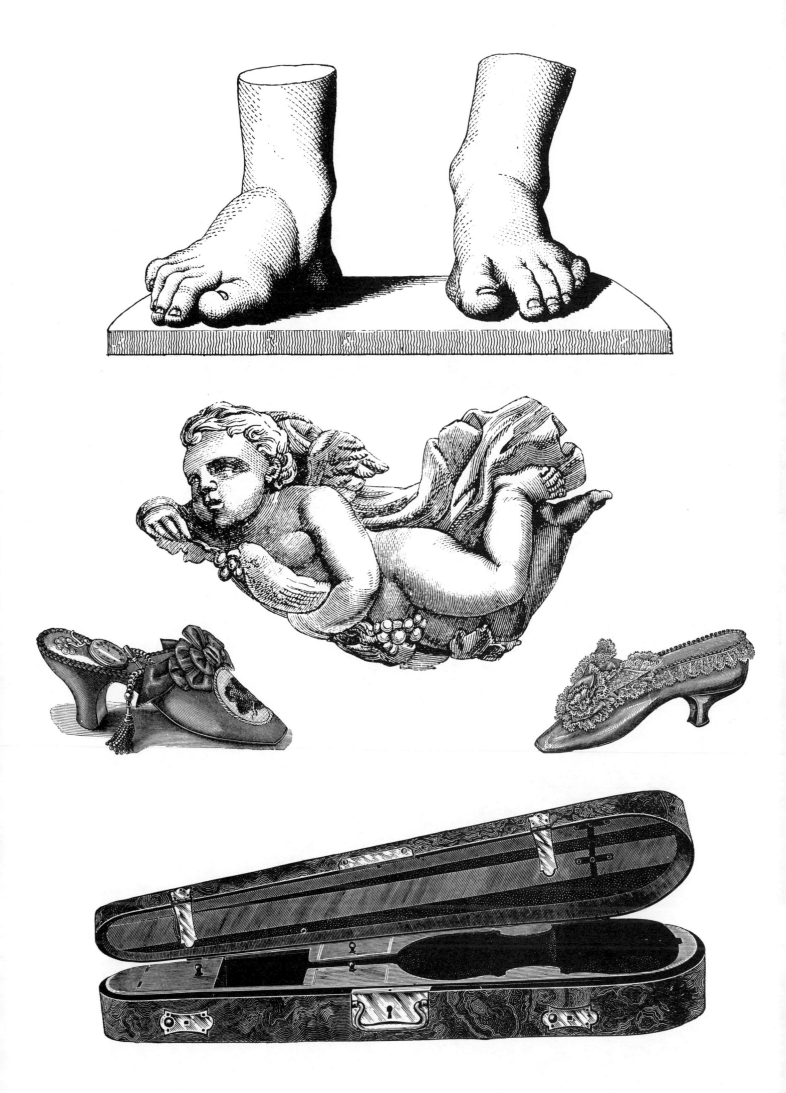

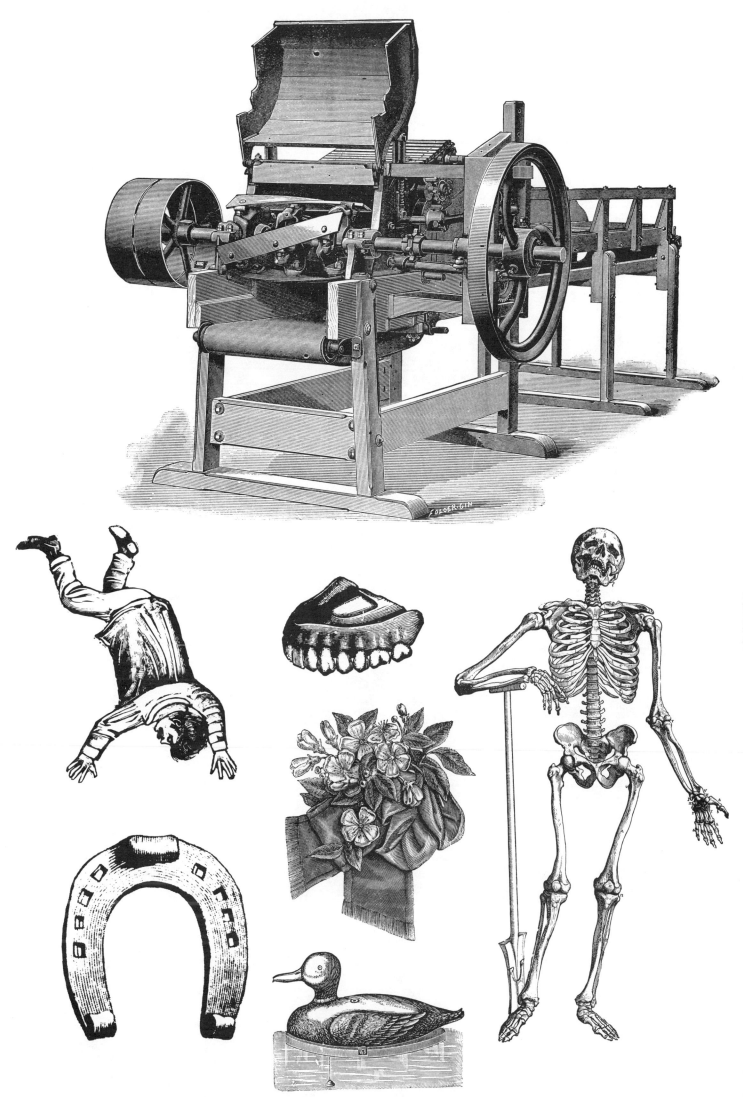